# Guide to Keap

I0466326

## Practical Guide

V. Telman

# Guide to Keap

# 1.Introduction to Keap

Keap is a marketing automation and customer management platform designed to help small and medium businesses grow and increase their productivity. With a particular focus on customer engagement and optimizing business processes, Keap offers a wide range of tools and features to help businesses manage their activities more efficiently and effectively.

The main goal of Keap is to simplify and automate marketing and customer management processes to allow businesses to focus on strategic activities and business growth. With an intuitive and user-friendly interface, Keap allows businesses to create and manage personalized marketing campaigns, automate sales processes, and provide excellent customer service.

One of Keap's distinctive features is its ability to integrate various functionalities and tools into one platform, allowing businesses to easily manage all their marketing and customer management activities in one place. With Keap, businesses can create and send personalized email marketing campaigns, manage customer contacts, track customer interactions, and efficiently automate sales processes.

Keap also offers advanced features for lead generation, managing sales opportunities, and creating analytical reports to monitor the performance of marketing and sales campaigns. With Keap, businesses can get a comprehensive view of their customers and marketing activities, allowing them to make informed decisions and continuously improve their marketing and sales strategies.

Additionally, Keap also provides dedicated customer service and a wide range of resources and support tools to help businesses get the most value out of the platform. With a team of marketing and sales experts available to provide personalized advice and assistance, Keap is committed to supporting businesses in achieving their growth and success goals.


In summary, Keap is a comprehensive solution for businesses looking to improve their marketing and customer management activities efficiently and effectively. With its wide range of tools and features, Keap offers businesses the opportunity for marketing automation and customer management to help them grow and thrive in today's competitive market.

## 2. Benefits of Using Keap

Keap is a customer management (CRM) and marketing automation software that offers a wide range of features designed to help small businesses manage their customers more efficiently and maximize their marketing potential. There are many benefits to using Keap to manage your business, and in this article, we will explore some of the key advantages that this software can offer.

One of the main benefits of using Keap is its ability to help you organize and manage your customers effectively. With Keap, you can easily keep track of all important information about your customers, such as their contact details, purchase history, and previous communications. This allows you to always have the information you need to provide personalized and quality service to your customers.

Additionally, Keap allows you to easily segment your customers based on various criteria, such as purchasing preferences, online behavior, and more. This enables you to send targeted and personalized communications to different segments of your customers, helping you maximize the effectiveness of your marketing campaigns and improve customer engagement.

Another key advantage of using Keap is its ability to automate many marketing and customer management tasks that would otherwise require significant time and resources. With Keap, you can create automated workflows that allow you to automatically send welcome messages to new customers, remind users to complete an abandoned purchase, and much more. This not only saves you time and effort but also helps ensure no sales opportunities are missed due to poor customer management.

Keap also allows you to easily create landing pages, signup forms, and other lead generation resources that help you capture new contacts and grow your list of potential customers. You can also track user behavior on your website and social channels to identify new sales opportunities and adjust your marketing strategies accordingly.

Another advantage of using Keap is its ability to provide in-depth analytics and detailed reports on the performance of your marketing campaigns and customer management. With Keap, you can closely monitor email open rates, click-through rates, conversions, and more, allowing you to quickly identify what is and isn't working in your marketing campaigns. This allows you to constantly adapt and optimize your strategies to maximize results and get the most value from your marketing efforts.

Lastly, another significant advantage of using Keap is its ease of use and flexibility. Keap is designed with an intuitive and user-friendly interface that allows you to easily manage all your marketing and customer management activities without the need for advanced technical skills. Additionally, Keap offers a wide range of features and customization options that allow you to tailor the software to the specific needs of your business and achieve the desired results.

Using Keap to manage your business offers a number of significant benefits that can help improve the efficiency of your operations, maximize customer engagement, and achieve better results from your marketing efforts. With its advanced features and user-friendly interface, Keap is a powerful solution for small businesses looking to expand their business and build lasting relationships with their customers. If you are looking for a way to improve customer management and marketing for your business, Keap could be the ideal solution for you.

## 3.Registration and Account Creation to Use Keap

Keap is a customer management and marketing automation software that allows businesses to organize, track, and automate many of the daily activities related to sales and marketing. To make the most of all the features offered by Keap, you need to create an account and sign up for the platform following a few simple steps.

The first step to start using Keap is to go to the official website of the platform and click on the "Sign Up" button. Once you have done that, you will be asked to enter some basic information such as your name, your email address, and a password that you will use to access your account. Make sure to choose a secure password, containing at least eight characters and a combination of letters, numbers, and special characters.

After entering the required information, a confirmation email will be sent to the address you provided during registration. Open the email and click on the confirmation link to confirm your registration and complete the process of creating your Keap account.

Once your registration is confirmed, you can access your Keap account using the email address and password you chose during registration. After logging in, you will be asked to complete your account profile by entering additional information such as your company name, industry sector, and other useful information to personalize your Keap experience.

After completing your account profile, you can start exploring all the features offered by Keap and using them to manage your customers, automate your marketing activities, and improve the performance of your sales campaigns. Keap offers a wide range of tools and resources to help you get the best possible results from the platform, so make sure to explore them all and make the most of Keap's potential for your business success.

Once you have created your account and completed your profile, you can start using

Keap's features to manage your customers, monitor your sales performance, and automate many of the daily tasks related to marketing and customer management. Keap allows you to create personalized marketing campaigns, track the results of your campaigns, and manage your customers effectively and organized.

Thanks to the powerful features offered by Keap, you can improve the efficiency of your marketing and sales activities, increase your performance, and achieve greater success for your business. By using Keap strategically and effectively, you can achieve tangible and concrete results for the growth and development of your business.

Creating an account and signing up for Keap is a simple and quick process that will give you access to a wide range of tools and resources to manage your customers, automate your marketing activities, and improve the performance of your sales campaigns. Make sure to complete your account profile and explore all the features offered by Keap to achieve the best results possible for your business.

# 4. Main menu and submenu of Keap

With a well-structured main menu and submenu, Keap makes it easy for users to access all the features and services offered by the platform.

Keap's main menu is divided into different main sections, each of which contains a series of options and tools to help users navigate and use the software efficiently. Within each main section, there are additional submenus that provide access to specific and detailed functions.

Here is a detailed overview of Keap's main menu and its submenus:

1. Dashboard: This section provides a comprehensive overview of ongoing activities, business performance, and key metrics. Here, users can view sales numbers, acquired contacts, ongoing marketing campaigns, and other important information. Submenus of this section include:

- Main Dashboard: Shows a complete overview of ongoing activities, key metrics, and business performance.
- Reports: Provides detailed reports and analysis of business performance, including sales data, marketing data, and customer interactions.
- Alerts: Notifications about important events and actions to be taken to improve business performance.

2. Contact Management: In this section, users can manage their contacts, including customers, prospects, and leads. Here, users can add, edit, and delete contacts, as well as monitor past and future interactions with each contact. Submenus of this section include:

- Contact List: Displays a complete list of contacts, including details such as name, email address, phone number, and more.
- Add Contact: To add new contacts to the database, with detailed information such as name, address, interests, and more.
- Import Contacts: To import an existing contact list from another software or service.

3. Marketing Automation: This section allows users to create and manage automated marketing campaigns, autoresponders, follow-up emails, and other marketing activities. Submenus of this section include:

- Marketing Campaigns: To create automated marketing campaigns, including email messages, SMS messages, and online advertising.
- Autoresponders: To create automatic messages that are sent to contacts based on specific actions or triggers.
- Contact Segmentation: To divide contacts into specific groups based on certain criteria or behaviors.

4. Sales: In this section, users can manage the sales process, create quotes, track sales opportunities, and manage contacts interested in the company's products or services. Submenus of this section include:

- Quotes: To create customized quotes for potential customers, including details about products, prices, and sales terms.
- Sales Opportunities: To manage ongoing

sales opportunities, track the status of negotiations, and monitor progress.

- Sales Pipeline: View the various stages of the sales process and monitor the progression of opportunities through the pipeline.

5. Reporting: This section provides detailed reports on business performance, including sales data, marketing data, customer interactions, and more. Submenus of this section include:

- Sales Reports: To view sales data, including sales charts, profit margins, sales trends, and more.
- Marketing Reports: To monitor the effectiveness of marketing campaigns, conversions, email open rates, and more.
- User Reports: To analyze user usage of the software, individual performance, and more.

6. Settings: In this section, users can customize their account settings, change notification preferences, update company information, and more. Submenus of this section include:

- Account: Edit personal information, password, and account security settings.
- Business Settings: Edit company information, including name, logo, address, and other contact information.
- Notification Preferences: Customize notifications and alerts about ongoing activities, sales opportunities, and more.

Keap's main menu and submenus are designed in a simple and intuitive way to allow users to quickly access the functionalities they need and use the software efficiently. With a well-organized structure and clear navigation, Keap makes it easy to manage business activities and helps companies grow and thrive in today's competitive market.

## 5.Contact Management

Keap is a contact management and customer relationship software designed to help small businesses organize and automate sales and marketing processes. With Keap, businesses can keep track of their contacts, manage customer communications, and create effective marketing campaigns to increase sales.

Contact management is a fundamental part of Keap's software, allowing users to store all important information about their customers in one place. With Keap, it is possible to create detailed profiles for each contact, including personal data, contact information, purchase history, past communications, and more. This way, users can have a complete and up-to-date view of each customer and interact with them in a more personalized and effective manner.

Keap also offers a range of tools to effectively manage contacts. For example, contacts can be organized into lists and segments based on specific criteria such as interests, buying behavior, or past interactions. This enables users to send targeted and personalized messages to different customer segments, thus increasing the chances of successful marketing campaigns.

Additionally, Keap allows users to automate many contact management tasks. For instance, users can set up automated workflows to automatically send follow-up messages, appointment reminders, or personalized offers based on customer actions. This not only saves time and effort, but also ensures that no contact is overlooked and that all customer interactions are timely and relevant.

Contact management in Keap extends beyond active customers to potential contacts and leads as well. Keap provides tools to capture and qualify leads in order to turn them into actual customers. For example, users can create custom contact forms to integrate on their website or other online platforms to collect information about potential customers and automatically initiate the follow-up process.

Keap also facilitates communication with contacts through various channels. For example, users can send personalized emails, SMS messages, push notifications, and more directly from Keap. This allows users to maintain constant contact with customers and communicate quickly and effectively, thereby increasing engagement and loyalty.

Furthermore, Keap offers advanced tools to analyze and monitor interactions with contacts. Users can track important metrics such as email open rates, link clicks, conversions, and more to evaluate the effectiveness of their marketing and sales strategies. This information can be used to optimize future campaigns and improve overall business performance.

Lastly, Keap helps protect contact data securely and in compliance with privacy regulations. Customer data is encrypted and stored securely in the cloud, ensuring maximum protection and confidentiality. Keap is also GDPR compliant and adheres to other privacy regulations, ensuring that contact data is handled legally and ethically. Contact management in Keap is a crucial element for the success of small businesses. With Keap, users can efficiently and effectively organize, automate, and optimize all customer interactions. With its wide range of features and advanced tools, Keap helps businesses build stronger relationships with customers, increase sales, and enhance their reputation in the market.

# 6. Creation of Marketing Campaigns

Keap (formerly known as Infusionsoft) is a marketing automation platform that allows businesses to effectively create and manage their marketing campaigns. With its advanced features, Keap enables the automation of customer acquisition, management, and retention processes, ensuring high efficiency and a greater return on investment.

The creation of marketing campaigns with Keap can be divided into different phases, each of which requires careful planning and execution. Below, we will see in detail how to use Keap to successfully create and manage your marketing campaigns.

Defining goals

Before starting to create a marketing campaign with Keap, it is crucial to clearly define the goals you want to achieve. These goals can vary depending on the company's marketing strategy, and may include increasing sales, acquiring new customers, retaining existing customers, or improving brand awareness. Once the goals are defined, it will be easier to plan and implement the activities needed to achieve them.

Analysis of the target audience

Once the marketing goals have been defined, it is essential to identify the target audience for the campaign. With Keap, you can create customer segments based on various criteria, such as age, gender, geographic location, or purchasing behavior. This segmentation allows for sending personalized and targeted messages, increasing the effectiveness of marketing campaigns and improving engagement with the audience.

Content creation

Another crucial phase in creating marketing campaigns with Keap is content production. This can include emails, SMS messages, landing pages, contact forms, surveys, or promotions. It is important that the content is relevant, high-quality, and consistent with the brand's image and values. Keap offers advanced tools for content creation and customization, allowing you to effectively reach your target audience.

Process automation

Thanks to Keap's marketing automation features, it is possible to automate various marketing processes, such as email sending, contact management, or tracking customer interactions. This automation saves time and resources, improving the efficiency of marketing campaigns and allowing you to focus on more strategic activities.

Monitoring and analysis of results

Once the marketing campaign is launched, it is essential to monitor and analyze the results obtained in order to evaluate its effectiveness and make any necessary changes. Keap provides advanced tools for monitoring campaign performance, allowing you to track metrics such as email open rate, click-through rate, conversions, or ROI. These data allow you to evaluate the campaign's effectiveness and optimize it in real-time to maximize results.

## Customer experience personalization

With Keap's advanced features, it is possible to personalize the customer experience to offer targeted and relevant messages based on each customer's specific needs and preferences. This personalization helps improve customer engagement and increase brand loyalty, contributing to building lasting and meaningful relationships with the target audience.

## Integration with other marketing tools

Keap can be integrated with other marketing and CRM tools to improve the management and automation of marketing campaigns. These integrations allow data synchronization between different platforms, optimizing processes and improving the user experience. Some popular integrations include WordPress, Shopify, WooCommerce, Salesforce, Google Analytics, and Facebook Ads.

## Best practices for successful marketing

campaigns with Keap

To maximize the results of marketing campaigns with Keap, it is important to follow some best practices that can help optimize the effectiveness of marketing activities. Some useful tips include:

- Carefully plan marketing activities, defining clear and measurable goals
- Segment the target audience based on specific criteria to send targeted and personalized messages
- Create quality and relevant content consistent with the brand image
- Automate marketing processes to save time and improve efficiency
- Constantly monitor the results of marketing campaigns and make any necessary changes in real-time
- Personalize the customer experience to increase engagement and loyalty
- Integrate Keap with other marketing and CRM tools to optimize processes and improve the user experience

Creating marketing campaigns with Keap can

be a complex process that requires planning, creativity, and careful result analysis. However, thanks to Keap's advanced features and its ability to automate marketing processes, significant results can be achieved and the return on investment can be maximized. By following best practices and leveraging the capabilities of Keap, businesses can create effective marketing campaigns that help achieve business goals and strengthen their positioning in the market.

# 7. Automation of processes

Keap is a process automation platform that offers solutions to manage customer relationships, automate marketing and sales processes, and improve the operational efficiency of a company. With its advanced features and user-friendly interface, Keap has become a popular choice among small and medium-sized businesses looking to streamline and optimize their operations.

One of Keap's key features is its contact management system, which allows businesses to keep all customer and lead information up-to-date and organized in a centralized database. This enables companies to have a complete and detailed view of their interactions with customers, improving communication and personalization of marketing and sales activities.

By automating marketing processes, Keap enables businesses to create customized workflows that are triggered by customer actions or predefined triggers. For example, a company can set up a workflow that automatically sends a series of follow-up emails to new leads or activates a promotional campaign when a customer makes a purchase. This helps businesses save time and energy, while also enhancing the effectiveness of their marketing strategies.

Additionally, Keap offers advanced tools for sales management, allowing businesses to track customer interactions, monitor sales opportunities, and manage customer acquisition and retention processes. Through its integration with online payment systems and management tools, Keap enables businesses to automate billing processes, manage contracts, and monitor sales performance in real time.

Keap can integrate with a wide range of other platforms and tools, allowing businesses to centralize and optimize their operations in a single dashboard. For example, Keap can be integrated with external CRM systems, e-commerce platforms, email marketing tools, and human resource management applications, enabling businesses to sync and automate their processes efficiently.

Thanks to its flexibility and scalability, Keap caters to the needs of businesses of any industry and size, allowing them to customize and optimize the platform according to their specific needs and business goals. With Keap, businesses can enhance the quality of service they offer to customers, increase sales and customer loyalty, and optimize their operations effectively and efficiently.

Process automation with Keap offers businesses the opportunity to simplify and optimize their operations, improve communication and personalization of marketing and sales activities, and increase overall productivity and efficiency of the organization. With its advanced features, ease of use, and ability to integrate with other platforms and tools, Keap stands as a comprehensive and reliable solution for companies looking to enhance their performance and success in the market.

# 8.Creating Email Templates with Keap

Creating email templates with Keap is a simple yet powerful process that allows businesses to create personalized and engaging messages for their audience. These templates can be used to send newsletters, promotions, event notifications, and more.

Before starting to create an email template with Keap, it is important to identify your target audience and the message you want to communicate. Once this is clarified, you can proceed with creating the template.

The first step is to choose a design and style that reflect the brand image. Keap offers a wide range of pre-designed templates that can be customized with your own logo, colors, and text. You can also create custom templates from scratch using Keap's drag-and-drop editor.

Once you have chosen the design of the template, you can add text, images, call-to-action buttons, and more. It is important to ensure that the text is clear, concise, and relevant to the target audience. Additionally, using high-quality images that capture the reader's attention is advisable.

Keap also offers the ability to personalize email templates using your contact data. For example, you can insert the recipient's name in the email body to make it more personal and engaging. Furthermore, you can segment your contacts based on specific criteria and send them personalized messages based on those criteria.

Once the email template creation is complete, you can test its effectiveness using Keap's A/B testing feature. This way, you can compare two versions of the template and determine which generates the most engagement with your contacts.

Finally, once the email template has been tested and optimized, you can use it to send email marketing campaigns to your contacts. Keap offers email tracking features that allow you to monitor the open, click, and other engagement metrics of your campaigns. These data are valuable for evaluating the effectiveness of your email marketing strategies and making any necessary changes to improve results.

Creating email templates with Keap is a fundamental process for businesses looking to effectively communicate with their customers. Whether using Keap's pre-designed templates or creating custom ones, you can create engaging and personalized messages that help keep contacts informed and interested in your offerings. With Keap's testing and tracking features, you can evaluate the effectiveness of your email marketing campaigns and make the necessary changes to achieve better results.

# 9.Monitoring performance with Keap

Keap is a customer management and marketing automation platform that offers a range of tools to monitor the performance of your business. Thanks to the numerous features provided by Keap, you can keep track of all aspects of your business activities and identify areas for improvement.

Monitoring performance with Keap is a fundamental process to ensure the success of your business. Through this platform, you can view real-time data related to sales, contacts, marketing campaigns, and much more. This allows you to have a complete overview of ongoing activities and make informed decisions to improve business performance.

One of the main tools offered by Keap for performance monitoring is the Customer Relationship Management (CRM) system, which allows you to organize and track all customer interactions. With Keap's CRM, you can efficiently manage and organize contacts, communications, sales, and customer activities. This helps you to effectively manage customer relationships and improve business performance.

In addition to CRM, Keap also offers tools for monitoring the performance of marketing campaigns. With Keap, you can create and monitor automated marketing campaigns that effectively reach a wide audience of potential customers. These campaigns can be monitored in real-time to evaluate the effectiveness of marketing strategies and make any necessary adjustments for better results.

Thanks to its seamless integration with other marketing platforms and tools, Keap allows you to monitor the performance of your business activities in detail. You can view all data related to sales, conversions, website traffic, and more to have a comprehensive overview of your business performance.

Another important tool offered by Keap for performance monitoring is the customizable dashboard, which allows you to clearly and intuitively visualize key data related to your business activities. Through Keap's dashboard, you can get a snapshot of your business performance and quickly identify any critical issues to address.

Keap also offers the ability to create detailed and customized reports to monitor your business performance over time. With Keap's reports, you can analyze data thoroughly and identify trends and patterns that may impact business performance. These reports can be shared with your team for better collaboration and planning of future strategies.

Monitoring performance with Keap is a crucial process to ensure the success of your business. With the numerous features offered by this platform, you can monitor all business activities and quickly identify areas for improvement. With Keap, you can monitor your business performance in detail to make informed decisions and achieve better results.

# 10. Using Analytical Reports with Keap

Analytical reports are a fundamental tool for monitoring a company's performance. With Keap, a management software for small businesses, it is possible to use a wide range of analytical reports to evaluate the effectiveness of your marketing, sales, and customer management strategies.

Keap offers a series of predefined reports that provide detailed information on contacts, sales opportunities, sent emails, and much more. These reports can be customized according to the specific needs of the company, allowing you to focus on the most relevant data for your business.

One of the most useful reports offered by Keap is the marketing campaign performance report. This report provides detailed information on emails sent, clicks, opens, and conversions generated by each marketing campaign. This allows you to evaluate the effectiveness of your marketing strategies and make any necessary changes to optimize results.

Another crucial report offered by Keap is the sales opportunity report. This report provides information on ongoing sales opportunities, conversions, average sales value, and more. With this report, you can closely monitor the sales process, identify areas for improvement, and make informed decisions to increase company revenue.

Keap's analytical reports also allow you to assess customer satisfaction and identify potential service issues. Through reports on customer interactions, you can monitor customer feedback, reviews, and complaints and quickly resolve any issues. Additionally, reports on appointments and planned activities help monitor team productivity and ensure that no opportunities are overlooked.

In addition to predefined reports, Keap offers the ability to create customized reports based on the specific needs of the company. This allows you to focus on the most relevant data for your business and obtain detailed information to support strategic decisions.

To use Keap's analytical reports, you need to follow a few simple steps. Firstly, access the dedicated area for reports within the software. Here, you can view predefined reports and create new customized reports.

Once you have selected the report of interest, you can choose the data to analyze and define filters to obtain more detailed information. For example, you can filter contacts based on acquisition source, contact date, or ongoing contract value.

Once the report is generated, you can view the data in various formats, including graphs, tables, and pie charts. This allows you to get a clear and intuitive overview of the information and easily identify any trends or anomalies.

Using analytical reports with Keap allows small businesses to closely monitor their performance, evaluate the effectiveness of their strategies, and make informed decisions to optimize results. With a wide range of reports and the ability to customize them to meet your specific needs, Keap proves to be an indispensable tool for business success.

## 11. How to improve your marketing strategy with Keap by Infusionsoft

Keap by Infusionsoft is a marketing automation platform that provides users with a variety of tools to enhance and optimize their marketing strategies. With its wide range of features, Keap allows businesses to efficiently manage their marketing activities, automate processes, and achieve tangible results.

One key to improving your marketing strategy with Keap is to fully leverage all of its features and integrate them into your overall marketing strategy. Here are some tips on how to make the most of Keap and enhance your marketing strategy.

1. Contact segmentation: One of Keap's most powerful features is the ability to segment contacts based on various criteria, such as interests, behaviors, past purchases, and more. By using segmentation, you can send targeted and personalized messages to users based on their preferences and behaviors, increasing the likelihood of success for your marketing

campaigns.

2. Process automation: Keap allows you to automate a variety of marketing processes, such as sending follow-up emails, lead management, and more. By using Keap's automated workflows, you can save time and resources, improve the efficiency of your marketing strategy, and ensure that no opportunities are missed.

3. Lead scoring: With Keap, you can assign a score to your leads based on their behavior, engagement level, and other factors. This allows you to identify the most promising leads and focus your marketing efforts on them, thereby increasing the chances of conversion.

4. Message personalization: By utilizing data collected by Keap, you can personalize your marketing messages based on the preferences, interests, and behaviors of your contacts. Message personalization can increase user engagement and improve the effectiveness of your marketing campaigns.

5. Monitoring and reporting: Keap offers advanced tools for monitoring the performance of your marketing campaigns and generating detailed reports on the effectiveness of your strategies. By using the data collected by Keap, you can identify areas that need improvement and make necessary changes to optimize your marketing strategies.

6. Integrations with other platforms: Keap offers the ability to integrate with other marketing platforms, such as social media, CRM, and analytics. By using these integrations, you can maximize the effectiveness of your marketing strategy and achieve tangible results.

7. Training and support: Keap provides training and support services for users, allowing you to fully understand the platform's features and receive assistance when needed. By taking full advantage of Keap's training and support services, you can maximize the effectiveness of your marketing strategy and achieve tangible results.

By fully utilizing the features and resources

offered by Keap by Infusionsoft, you can significantly improve your marketing strategy, increase the effectiveness of your campaigns, and achieve tangible results. By leveraging contact segmentation, process automation, lead scoring, message personalization, monitoring and reporting, integrations with other platforms, and the training and support services offered by Keap, you can create more effective and successful marketing strategies.

## 12. Keap integrates with other platforms

Keap is a marketing automation and customer management platform that offers a range of tools and features to simplify marketing activities and customer relationship management. One of the most appreciated features of Keap is its ability to integrate with other platforms and applications, allowing users to easily synchronize data and automate marketing and sales processes.

Integration with other platforms is a key element in getting the most value from Keap and fully utilizing its capabilities. By integrating with other platforms, users can expand Keap's functionalities and connect it with other tools and services used in marketing and customer management. This helps improve efficiency, optimize processes, and ensure a better overall experience for customers.

Keap offers a series of pre-built integrations with various popular platforms and services, such as Google Ads, Facebook Ads,

Mailchimp, Zapier, WordPress, QuickBooks, PayPal, and many others. These integrations allow for easy data synchronization between Keap and other platforms, automate processes, and create customized workflows to meet specific business needs.

To integrate Keap with other platforms, users can use the dedicated "Integrations" section within the Keap dashboard. Here, users can search among the available integrations and activate those necessary for their business. Once the desired integrations are activated, users can configure them according to their needs and start synchronizing data between Keap and other platforms.

Integrations with other platforms offer several advantages for businesses using Keap. Firstly, they help centralize data in one platform, making it easier to manage and analyze customer information. Additionally, integrations help automate marketing and sales processes, saving time and resources, and improving the overall efficiency of the company.

Thanks to integrations with other platforms, users can create automated and customized workflows that allow for targeted marketing messages, more effective lead management, monitoring of advertising campaign performances, and much more. Additionally, integrations allow for a more comprehensive view of customers by integrating data from various sources and improving the quality of available information.

Integrations with other platforms also offer the opportunity to make the most of Keap's features, expanding the platform's capabilities and allowing for customization to adapt to specific business needs. Through integrations, users can integrate Keap with advanced analytics tools, online payment systems, e-commerce platforms, and more, allowing them to create comprehensive and highly customized solutions to effectively manage marketing and sales activities.

Integration with other platforms is a fundamental element in getting the most value from Keap and fully utilizing its capabilities. By integrating with other platforms, users can centralize data, automate processes, improve efficiency, and create customized solutions to optimize marketing and customer management activities. To maximize the effectiveness of Keap and achieve tangible results in their business, it is essential to explore the various integrations available and make the most of the platform's features.

# 13. Customization of automatic responses with Keap

Keap is a marketing automation and customer management platform that allows you to customize automatic responses in order to create more effective and personalized communication with customers. Thanks to Keap's features, you can create automatic responses that take into account customers' preferences and behaviors, in order to offer them a personalized and relevant experience.

For example, imagine you have an online clothing store and use Keap to manage your customer contacts. With Keap, you can create automatic responses that are sent to customers based on the actions they take on your website or the information they provide during registration.

If a customer visits your website and adds some products to their cart but doesn't complete the purchase, you can use Keap to automatically send a follow-up email encouraging them to complete the purchase.

In this email, you can also include suggestions for other products that may interest them, based on the products they added to their cart.

Furthermore, if a customer subscribes to your newsletter or fills out a contact form on your website, you can use Keap to automatically send a welcome email thanking them for subscribing and providing further information about your products and services.

Keap also allows you to segment your contacts based on certain criteria, such as age, gender, or purchasing preferences, in order to send even more personalized and targeted automatic responses. For example, if you have a special promotion for customers aged 25-35, you can use Keap to automatically send a promotion email only to those customers within that age group.

Additionally, Keap allows you to track customer interactions with your automatic responses, in order to evaluate the effectiveness of your marketing strategies and make any necessary changes to improve results. For example, you can monitor email open rates, click-through rates, and sales conversions generated by automatic responses sent with Keap, to understand which messages work best and optimize your marketing campaigns based on the results obtained.

Customizing automatic responses with Keap is a great strategy to improve the effectiveness of your customer communications and offer them a more personalized and engaging shopping experience. With Keap's advanced features, you can create targeted automatic responses based on your customers' behavior and preferences, thus improving your marketing strategy and increasing conversions and sales for your business.

## 14. Managing contacts

With Keap, you can create, segment, and automate contacts with potential customers in order to guide them through the buying process and convert them into satisfied customers.

To create a funnel with Keap, you need to follow some essential steps that will help you optimize the sales process and improve the performance of your marketing strategy. Here's how to do it:

1. Setting goals: before starting to create your funnel with Keap, it is important to establish clear marketing and sales goals. Define what goals you want to achieve with your funnel, such as increasing sales, acquiring new customers, or retaining existing ones.

2. Identifying the target market: once the goals have been defined, it is necessary to identify your target market. Who are your potential customers? What are their needs and interests? Defining your target market will help you

create targeted content and messages that will attract and engage your potential customers.

3. Creating valuable content: to attract and engage your potential customers, it is essential to create valuable content. Use Keap to create landing pages, email marketing, and social media content that is relevant and interesting to your audience. Offer them useful information, practical advice, and resources that can help them solve their problems and meet their needs.

4. Contact segmentation: once you have caught the attention of your potential customers, it is important to segment your contacts based on their characteristics and behaviors. Use Keap to create contact lists based on user activities, interests, and interactions with your company. This way, you can send personalized and targeted messages that meet the specific needs of each audience segment.

5. Automating marketing activities: to effectively manage your sales funnel, it is necessary to automate marketing activities.

Use Keap to create automated workflows that send follow-up messages, special offers, and promotions to your potential customers based on their interactions with your company. This way, you can maintain constant contact with your customers and guide them through the buying process.

6. Analyzing results: finally, it is essential to monitor and analyze the results of your sales funnel. Use Keap to track conversions, measure the performance of your marketing campaigns, and identify areas for improvement. Modify and optimize your strategies based on the data collected to maximize your results and achieve a positive ROI.

To give you a more concrete idea of how to create and manage a funnel with Keap, here is a practical example:

Imagine you manage an online clothing company and want to create a funnel to increase sales of your new arrivals. Here's how you could proceed with Keap:

1. Setting goals: your goal is to increase sales of your online clothing company's new arrivals and acquire new customers interested in fashion.

2. Identifying the target market: your target market consists of men and women aged 18 to 35 interested in fashion and trends.

3. Creating valuable content: use Keap to create a landing page dedicated to your new arrivals with photos and detailed product descriptions. Also send email marketing with special promotions and post on social media to promote your new arrivals and engage your audience.

4. Contact segmentation: using Keap, create contact lists based on gender, age, and interests of potential customers interacting with your company. Send personalized messages and special offers based on the preferences of each audience segment.

5. Automating marketing activities: create automated workflows with Keap that send follow-up messages after purchase, special

offers for loyal customers, and reminders to stimulate the purchase of your new arrivals.

6. Analyzing the results: monitor conversions, email open rates, and social media interactions using Keap to identify the best-selling products, most effective strategies, and areas for improvement in your sales funnel.

By creating and managing a funnel with Keap in this way, you can effectively and automatically increase sales of your online clothing company's new arrivals and acquire new customers interested in fashion.

## 15. Managing the sales force with Infusionsoft

Infusionsoft is a marketing automation and sales management platform that allows businesses to efficiently manage the sales process and improve the performance of their sales force. In this article, we will examine how to use Infusionsoft to effectively manage the sales force.

First of all, it is important to understand that the sales force is one of the crucial elements for the success of a company. It is the engine that drives sales and generates profits. But to ensure that the sales force is effective, it is essential that it is managed properly. Infusionsoft offers a range of tools and features that can help businesses manage their sales force more effectively.

One of the main advantages of Infusionsoft is its automation capability. Through automation, it is possible to significantly reduce the time and effort required to manage the sales force. For example, Infusionsoft allows you to automate the process of sending follow-up emails to potential customers, track sales activities, and generate detailed reports on the performance of the sales force.

Furthermore, Infusionsoft offers a range of sales management tools that can help improve the effectiveness of the sales force. For example, you can use Infusionsoft to track customer contacts, sales opportunities, and leads in a centralized system. This allows you to have a complete view of the sales pipeline and adopt more targeted strategies to convert leads into customers.

Another important feature of Infusionsoft is its ability to create and manage marketing and sales campaigns in a simple and intuitive way. With Infusionsoft, you can easily create personalized marketing emails, create effective landing pages, and plan sales campaigns efficiently. This allows the sales force to focus on the most important activities and achieve better results.

Infusionsoft also offers advanced analytics tools that allow you to monitor the performance of the sales force and identify areas that need improvement. For example, you can monitor the number of leads generated, conversion rate, and sales value for each salesperson. This allows you to identify the top-performing salespeople and adopt strategies to improve the performance of those who are less successful.

Finally, Infusionsoft offers a range of support and training tools that can help the sales force improve their skills and achieve their sales goals. For example, you can access webinars, tutorials, and educational resources that provide tips and suggestions on how to improve sales performance. Additionally, Infusionsoft offers a dedicated customer support service that can provide assistance and resolve any issues the sales force may encounter.

Infusionsoft is a powerful and flexible platform that can help businesses manage their sales force effectively. With its automation, sales management, and advanced analytics capabilities, Infusionsoft allows businesses to enhance the performance of their sales force and achieve better results. If used correctly, Infusionsoft can become a valuable ally for businesses looking to increase their sales and grow in the market.

## 16.Creating an e-commerce with Keap Infusionsoft

Creating an e-commerce with Keap Infusionsoft is a process that requires attention and care to ensure the success of your online store. Keap Infusionsoft is a marketing automation and CRM software platform that allows you to effectively manage your sales, marketing, and customer relationships.

Before starting to create your e-commerce with Keap Infusionsoft, it is important to plan and define your goals and sales strategies. You must have a clear understanding of your needs and requirements, so you can configure the platform appropriately and optimally.

The first step to create an e-commerce with Keap Infusionsoft is to sign up on the platform and create an account. Once registered, you can start configuring your online store. Keap Infusionsoft offers various options to customize your e-commerce, such as creating sales pages, integrating payment modules, managing products, and more.

To set up your e-commerce with Keap Infusionsoft, you will first need to add your products to the catalog. You can input detailed information about your products, such as images, descriptions, prices, and availability. Additionally, you can organize your products into categories and subcategories to facilitate customer navigation on your online store.

Once your product catalog is configured, you can create sales pages to promote and sell your products. Keap Infusionsoft's sales pages allow you to customize the design and layout, add purchase buttons, and integrate payment tools like PayPal, Stripe, or other online payment methods.

To increase conversions and sales in your e-commerce, you can use Keap Infusionsoft's marketing automation features. You can create automated marketing campaigns that send personalized messages to customers based on their purchasing behavior and interactions with your online store. This way, you can effectively engage customers and drive sales.

To manage customer relationships in your e-commerce, you can use Keap Infusionsoft's CRM. You can record customer information, track interactions with them, and send personalized communications to maintain a lasting and trusting relationship with your customers.

One of the most interesting features of Keap Infusionsoft is the ability to create customer loyalty programs. You can use loyalty points, exclusive discounts, and special promotions to reward loyal customers and encourage repeat purchases in your e-commerce.

Finally, to ensure an optimal shopping experience for your customers, it is essential to monitor and analyze the performance of your e-commerce with Keap Infusionsoft. You can use analytics and reporting tools to evaluate key metrics such as conversion rate, average order value, and website traffic, in order to identify areas for improvement and optimize your sales strategies.

Creating an e-commerce with Keap Infusionsoft is a unique opportunity to develop and manage a successful online store.

With powerful marketing automation, CRM, and sales management features, you can promote your products, engage customers, and increase sales effectively and efficiently. By following a well-defined strategy and customizing the platform to meet your needs, you can create a successful e-commerce that will allow you to grow and thrive in the online market.

# Index